SAILING THE MIRROR

Roy Partridge

Photographs by
Tim Hore

Fernhurst Books, London

First published 1980 by
Fernhurst Books, 13 Fernhurst Road, London SW6

ISBN 0 906754 01 1

Acknowledgements

The photographs for the cover and page 3 were
taken by Arthur Sidey.
    All other photographs for this book were taken
by Tim Hore at the Queen Mary Sailing Club,
Ashford, Middlesex.
    Thanks are due to Ivor Finn of the Bell
Woodworking Company for his advice on the
manuscript.

Composition by Allset, London
Printed by Hollen Street Press, Slough

Contents

1 Rigging 5
2 Sailing theory 6
3 A first sail 10
4 'Go-fast' gear 13
5 Launching 18
6 Reaching 20
7 Beating 25
8 Tacking 30
9 Running 34
10 Gybing 38
11 Capsizing 42
12 Landing 44
13 Tuning 46
14 The spinnaker 48
15 Racing 56

1 Burgee
2 Gaff
3 Main halyard
4 Jib halyard strop
5 Jib halyard
6 Gaff jaws
7 Jib
8 Forestay
9 Hanks
10 Bow
11 Buoyancy tanks
12 Forward and aft mast steps
13 Jibsheet
14 Fairlead
15 Forward and aft shroud anchorages
16 Shroud
17 Kicking strap (vang)
18 Centreboard
19 Boom
20 Gooseneck
21 Mast
22 Thwart
23 Tiller extension
24 Tiller
25 Rudder
26 Mainsheet
27 Stern/transom
28 Mainsail
29 Batten/batten pocket
30 Luff rope
31 Downhaul

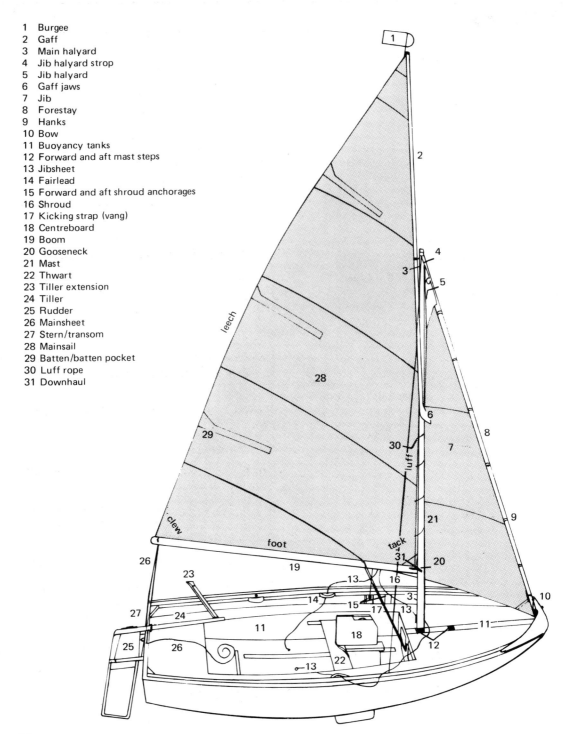

1.1

4

1 Rigging

The standard Mirror dinghy can be rigged in a few minutes—with a little practice! A sensible order for putting it together is given below. The boat should then look like the drawing on page 4.

Point the boat into the wind.

Loop the jib halyard strop over the top of the mast so the block hangs forward of the mast.

Loop the two shrouds over the top of the mast.

Loop the forestay over the top of the mast.

Attach the opposite ends of the shrouds to the aft (back) shroud anchorages.

Run gaff and jib halyards through their respective blocks at the top of the mast, the gaff from stern to bow and the jib from bow to stern.

Set the mast upright in the aft mast step.

Fasten the forestay to the forestay anchorage.

Loop the kicking strap (vang) over the boom.

Fasten the mainsheet (the rope controlling the mainsail) on the port side of the transom. Lead the mainsheet through the eye on the boom and back through the eye on the starboard side of the transom. Tie a 'figure-of-eight' knot in the end.

Attach the boom to the gooseneck.

Slide the mainsail up the gaff and fasten the peak of the sail to the top of the gaff with a short length of rope.

Insert the sail battens (thin end first) in their batten pockets.

Fasten the clew of the mainsail to the end of the boom with a short piece of rope. Tie a second piece through the clew and around the boom.

Wind the luff rope around the mast. Tie a second piece through the tack and around the mast.

Hoist the gaff tight to the mast.

Secure the downhaul and luff rope.

Push down on the boom and tighten the kicking strap (vang). Secure it to the fitting beneath the mast.

Attach the jib peak to the halyard and raise the jib slightly.

Attach the jib hanks to the forestay.

Fasten the jib tack to the forestay anchorage with a length of rope.

Fasten the jib sheets to the jib clew and lead back through the fairleads. Tie a figure-of-eight knot at the end of each jibsheet.

Hoist the jib fully. Make sure the halyard is tight.

Attach the rudder and tiller to the transom. Pull the rudder blade up and cleat the rope on the tiller.

Check the bungs are all in place in the buoyancy compartments.

When afloat, put in the centreboard and push down the rudder blade.

2 Sailing theory

Take a careful look at the photograph on this page. You will see that:

The helmsman sits on the windward side of the boat.

The helmsman always holds the tiller in his aft (back) hand. He steers with the tiller.

The helmsman always holds the mainsheet in his forward (front) hand. The mainsheet adjusts the angle of the mainsail to the centreline of the boat.

The crew uses his weight to help the helmsman prevent the boat heeling. This means sitting to windward in strong winds, to leeward in light winds.

The crew generally holds the jibsheet in his aft hand. The jibsheet controls the angle of the jib to the centreline of the boat.

The jib and mainsail are roughly parallel.

How does a boat sail?

Wind is a boat's driving force. The wind flows over the windward side of each sail (causing pressure) and round the leeward side (causing suction). The resulting force on the sails is in the direction of arrows A and B in Fig. 2.2, i.e. it is at right angles to each sail.

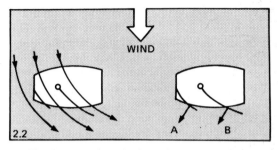

The force pushes the boat forwards and sideways. The forwards push propels the boat. The sideways push is counteracted by water pressure on the centreboard.

The helmsman's and crew's weight counteracts the turning (capsizing) effect. The further you lean out, the more leverage you get—this is called 'sitting out' or 'hiking'.

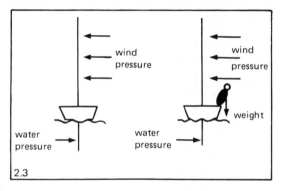

If the sails are pulled in, forces A and B will be almost at right angles to the boat: the sideways force is maximum and the centreboard

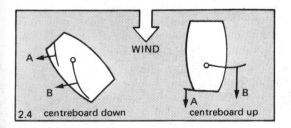

needs to be pushed right down to counteract it. If the sails are let out, the forces point forwards: there is no sideways force, so the centreboard can be pulled up.

How can I steer?

When a boat is sailing straight, the water flows past the rudder undisturbed. When the rudder is turned, the water is deflected. The water hitting the rudder pushes it, and the back of the boat, in direction C. The bow turns to the left.

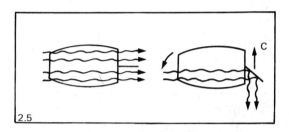

In short, pulling the tiller towards you turns the bow away from you, and vice versa.

How can I stop?

It is the wind in the sails that makes a boat go forward. To stop, take the wind out of the sails either by letting go of the sheets or by altering course towards the wind.

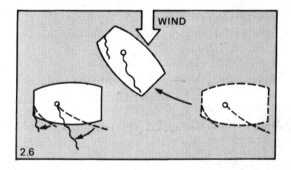

How can I tell which way the wind is blowing?

Everything in sailing is related to the wind direction. You can tell which way it's blowing by the feel of it on your cheek, by the wave direction or by using a burgee. Remember, the burgee points to where the wind is going.

POINTS OF SAILING

Look at Fig. 2.11 on the opposite page. There are three points of sailing:

1 *Reaching*—the boat sails *across* the wind (Fig. 2.7).
2 *Beating*—the boat sails *towards* the wind (Fig. 2.8).
3 *Running*—the boat sails with the wind *behind* (Fig. 2.9).

Reaching

The boat in Fig. 2.7 is reaching. It is sailing at right angles to the wind, which is blowing from behind the helmsman's back. The sails are about halfway out and the centreboard halfway up.

Beating

If you want to change course towards the wind, you must push the centreboard down and pull in the sails as you turn. You can go on turning towards the wind until the sails are pulled right in. Then you are *beating* (Fig. 2.8).

If you try to turn further towards the wind, you enter the 'no go area'. The sails flap and the boat stops.

To get from A to B, the only way is to *beat* in a zigzag fashion (Fig. 2.10).

At the end of each 'zig' the boat turns through an angle of 90°. This is called a *tack*. The boat

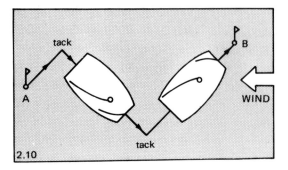

2.10

turns 'through' the wind—the sails blow across to the other side and the helmsman and crew must shift their weight across the boat to balance it.

Running

From a reach, you may want to change course away from the wind. Pull up the centreboard (not more than three-quarters up) and let out the sails as you turn. You can go on turning until the wind is coming from behind the boat. Then you are *running* (Fig. 2.9).

Note that the crew has pulled the jib across to the opposite side to the mainsail: this is called 'goosewinging' and is only used when running. If you turn more, the boat will gybe. The wind blows from the other side of the mainsail, which flicks across to the other side of the boat. Push the centreboard down before the gybe, and shift your weight as the boom comes across.

2.7

2.8

2.9

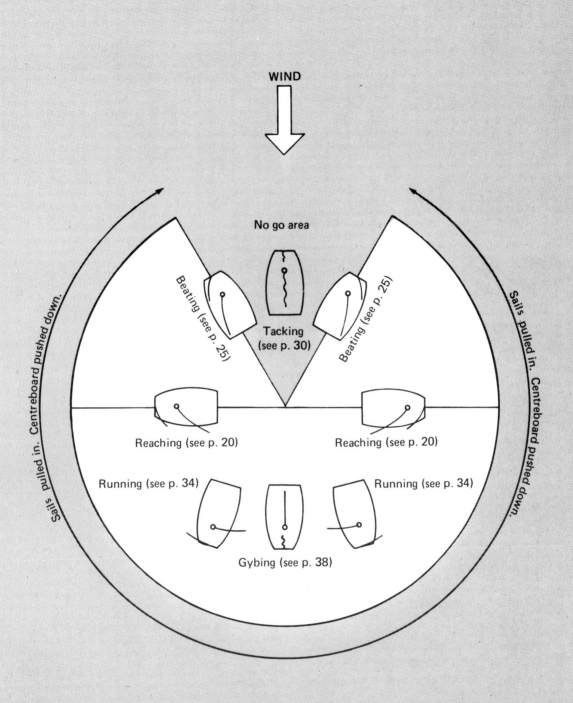

WIND

No go area

Beating (see p. 25)

Tacking
(see p. 30)

Beating (see p. 25)

Sails pulled in. Centreboard pushed down.

Sails pulled in. Centreboard pushed down.

Reaching (see p. 20)

Reaching (see p. 20)

Running (see p. 34)

Running (see p. 34)

Gybing (see p. 38)

2.11

3 A first sail

Try to choose a day with a gentle breeze for your first sail. Wind is measured either on the Beaufort scale or in metres per second. Force 4 or above would be unsuitable.

Wind speed

Beaufort number	Speed (knots)	Speed (metres per second)
0	1	0.5
1	1–3	0.6–1.9
2	4–6	2.0–3.5
3	7–10	3.6–5.9
4	11–16	6.0–9.4
5	17–21	9.5–12.4
6	22–27	12.5–15.9
7	28–33	16.0–19.5
8	34–40	19.6–23.5

A reservoir, river or estuary is a good place to learn to sail. If you are learning on the open sea, try to avoid an offshore wind (wind blowing from shore to sea)—you may get blown a long way from the shore. *Always* wear lifejackets, and stay with the boat whatever happens.

Rig the boat as described on pages 4 to 5, and launch as described on pages 18 and 19. As soon as you can, get sailing on a reach (Fig. 3.1) with the wind blowing at right angles to the boat. The centreboard will be about half up and the sails about half out.

The helmsman sits on the side opposite the sails. Practise adjusting the mainsheet and steering. Try to get the 'feel' of the boat, particularly using your weight to balance the wind in the sail.

The crew sits wherever is best to stop the boat heeling. Practise adjusting the jib, which should be roughly parallel to the mainsail. Move your body to help the helmsman keep the boat level. (Reaching is discussed in more detail on pages 20-24.)

Eventually you will need to tack (turn round—Fig. 3.2) and reach back again. Tacking is discussed on pages 30 and 31. The crew needs to let out the jibsheet and pull in the opposite one as you tack. Try to tack smoothly, changing sides as you do so. If the boat stops during a tack, keep the tiller central and wait until the boat starts to drift backwards. Eventually it will turn to one side and you'll be able to get sailing again.

Reach back and forth until you have gained confidence. Try picking an object and sailing straight towards it, adjusting the sheets so the sails are as far out as possible without flapping. If a gust comes, let the sheets out. Try to keep the boat moving.

Next try picking objects slightly closer to or slightly further away from the wind. Try sailing

3.1

towards them adjusting the sheets: the sheets should be pulled in more when sailing closer to the wind.

When you've had enough, head for the shore. If the wind is onshore, when you are about 50 metres away point the boat into the wind and let the mainsail down; then turn and drift ashore. If the wind is offshore, simply sail up to the shore letting go of the sheets as you get near. Don't forget to pull up the rudder and centre-board in good time. Landing is discussed in more detail on pages 44-5.

The next steps

When you feel happy reaching and tacking, you are ready to try the other points of sailing (see page 8).

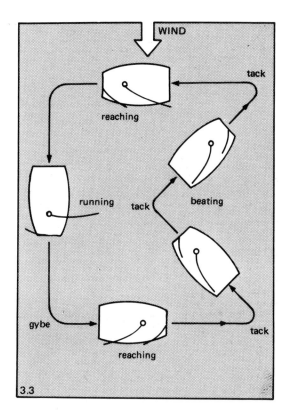

3.3

3.2

One good way to practise is to sail round a square 'course' (Fig. 3.3).

From your reach, gradually turn away from the wind, letting out the sails and pulling the centre-board three-quarters up. You are now running. After a while, push down the centreboard (to let the crew get across the boat), pull the tiller towards you and gybe. Now reach the other way, with the centreboard half down and the mainsheet half out. Next, push the centreboard right down and turn towards the wind, pulling in your sails. You are beating. Tack, and beat the other way. When you are far enough into the wind, turn off on to a reach, letting the sails out and pulling the centreboard half up. Try several laps.

Remember:

The helmsman sits on the windward side.

He keeps the mainsheet in his front hand, tiller in his back hand.

If you get out of control, let go of both main and jibsheets—don't panic!

11

4 'Go-fast' gear

If you are going to race your Mirror, you should consider fitting some or all of the accessories allowed by the class rules. These are fitted to the boat as shown in Fig. 4.1 opposite.

Chainplates

Chainplates (Figs. 4.2 and 4.3) can be fitted as attachments for the shrouds and forestay: they will

can hike comfortably. Note the shockcord to hold the helmsman's toestraps off the floor, so you can get your feet under them easily.

Compass

A tactical compass helps you spot windshifts (see page 62), particularly when sailing at sea. The compass in Fig. 4.5 is fitted on the thwart.

4.2

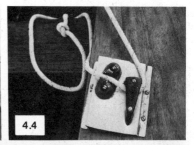

4.3

4.4

allow you to alter the rake of the mast, which is essential for tuning the boat (see page 46).

Jib cleats and fairleads

Jib cleats free the crew's hands for other jobs. The correct positioning of the fairleads is vital for speed to windward—p. 46 tells you how this is done. The cleat and fairlead are supported by a sheet of aluminium at an angle to make cleating easier (Fig. 4.4).

Self bailer

A self bailer (Fig. 4.5) will remove unwanted water when the boat is moving fast. Don't forget to pull it up before you come ashore!

Toestraps

A good way of fixing the toestraps is shown in Fig. 4.5. Adjust them so the helmsman and crew

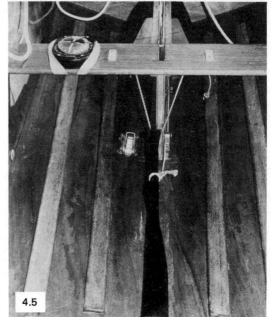

4.5

Gaff band

It is essential to be able to hoist the gaff tight to the mast. If you have a long-necked gaff band, replace it with a short-necked one—this will actually fit inside the sheave at the top of the mast when the gaff is fully hoisted.

Universal tiller joint

This fitting lets the tiller extension pivot in any direction.

Centreboard shockcord

A length of shockcord fitted over the centreboard case will keep the centreboard firmly in position. Fix the ends underneath the thwart on either side of the centreboard case. The shockcord goes over the centreboard when the board is fully down, and behind it when it is raised.

Rudder downhaul

Replace the elastic with rope led to a cleat on the tiller. Your rudder blade will then be held down firmly; this is particularly important in strong winds, when water pressure tends to force the blade up, making the boat hard to steer.

'Telltales'

Telltales are 12 cm lengths of wool fitted on the sails to indicate wind flow. You should position them 15 cm behind the centre of the jib luff: thread a needle with a 24 cm length of wool or terylene, push the needle through the jib until you have 12 cm on each side, then slide off the needle and knot the wool close to the sail on each side.

The helmsman uses the telltales to windward, steering close to the wind until the windward telltale begins to collapse. The crew uses them on a reach to set the jib—adjusting the jibsheet until the telltales on each side of the jib stream backwards.

Flexible top batten

A flexible top batten allows a gentle curve in the top of the mainsail.

Terylene jibsheets and mainsheet

Terylene sheets are stronger than cotton ones, so they can be a little thinner. They also last longer!

Mainsheet blocks

Replace the mainsheet fittings with blocks—one under the boom, the other on the transom. These cut down friction when you adjust the mainsheet.

Wire halyards

The best halyards for the jib and mainsail are made of wire, with rope 'tails' for cleating. These not only stretch less than rope halyards, but give less wind resistance. The main halyard should be as tight as possible. The jib halyard should be as tight as possible without causing a gully to form behind the luff.

Halyard cleats

Metal clam cleats at the foot of the mast are the best for cleating halyards. They prevent slipping and make for easy adjustment when under way (see Fig. 4.6).

An alternative is to loop the ends of the wire halyards over pegs or 'shark's teeth' set at the bottom of the mast; this system gives the minimum of halyard stretch in strong winds.

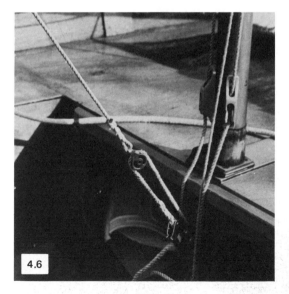

4.6

MAINSAIL CONTROLS

Apart from the mainsheet, three ropes control the shape of the mainsail. These are the kicking strap (vang), the outhaul and the downhaul.

The sail is cut so that it sets with a curve or belly. The larger the curve, the more drive the sail has, but the larger the heeling effect. Adjusting the sail controls alters the curve in the sail. The curve should be larger for reaching and running, smaller for beating and in strong winds.

The kicking strap pulls down on the boom. This stops the sail twisting, and also bends the gaff and mast, flattening the sail. The downhaul and outhaul also flatten the sail when pulled tight.

Kicking strap (vang)

The kicking strap or vang controls the twist in the back of the sail. It also controls the bend in the gaff and mast, which in turn affects the curve or belly in the sail. Fig. 4.7 shows the effect of a slack kicking strap. The sail is losing drive, and it is impossible to set it at the correct angle to the wind along its length. The sail is too far in at the bottom, and too far out at the top.

A pulley and cleat make adjusting the kicking strap much easier (Fig. 4.6). To set it, pull in the mainsheet fully; tighten the kicking strap and then release the mainsheet. This is 'normal' tension.

Paint a mark on each strand of the pulley rope so that the marks line up when you have 'normal' tension—this allows you to find the same setting every time. In strong winds, you need the kicking strap a little tighter than 'normal'. In very strong winds it should be bar tight.

In light winds, let the kicking strap off a little from 'normal'. It should be just firm enough to prevent the boom lifting. If it is too tight the mast and gaff will bend, and the sail will be too flat and may 'hook' to windward at the leech.

Unless the wind changes its strength, you need not adjust the kicking strap while you're sailing.

Outhaul

A simple method of rigging the outhaul is shown in Fig. 4.8. This gives a 2:1 purchase. The rope is led to a cleat close to the kicking strap block on the boom, which makes it easy to adjust on all points of sailing.

The outhaul controls the curve on the bottom part of the mainsail. If it is tight, the sail is flat. If it is loose, a powerful curve forms.

If you are beginners, you don't need to adjust the outhaul while sailing. More experienced sailors will tighten the outhaul when beating and loosen it when reaching—the clew will then be about 7 cm nearer the mast than when beating. When running, pull the outhaul fairly tight. In strong winds, have the outhaul tighter than in light winds. A loose setting will result in a gap of about 30 cm between the middle of the boom and the foot of the sail. In very strong winds, the setting should be bar tight. You may find it helpful to mark the track to help you remember a successful setting.

Letting out the mainsheet makes adjusting the outhaul easier; loosening the kicking strap makes it easier still.

4.7

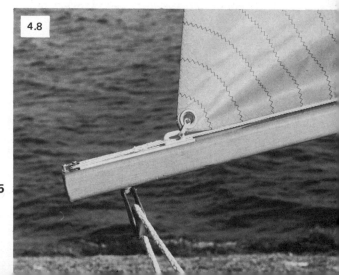

4.8

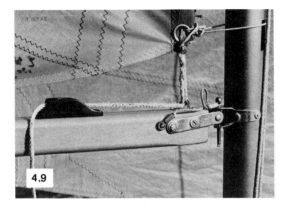

4.9

Downhaul

There are many ways of rigging a downhaul. A simple method giving a 2:1 purchase is shown in Fig. 4.9. The beginner might tighten it as much as possible with one hand and leave it set like this while sailing. More experienced sailors need to adjust the downhaul while afloat. The idea is to obtain the best aerofoil shape for drive. You will find you need more tension when beating than when reaching and running.

When beating, aim to have the maximum camber in the sail two-fifths of the way aft along the boom. The camber moves aft as the wind increases, so you need more tension on the downhaul to pull it forward again. When beating in strong winds, pull the downhaul as tight as possible.

When reaching or running, you also need more downhaul tension as the wind strength increases. Aim to just remove the horizontal creases in the front of the sail.

SPINNAKER GEAR

If you are going to race at all seriously, you will need a spinnaker. The class rules place very few restrictions on the type of spinnaker you can use, but check with the current yearbook to make sure you are in class—as you should with any other additions you make.

Briefly, the spinnaker is restricted by maximum size and by method of manufacture. The spinnaker pole is limited to a maximum length of 152.3 cm (5 feet) and the positioning of the fittings by the IYRU rules.

Because of the great flexibility allowed, the following list of items you will need is only suggested as a guide.

Spinnaker
Spinnaker boom and support rod (or rope and elastic downhaul with clam cleat)
2 spinnaker boom brackets (mount one on the forward side of the mast, the other in the middle of the foredeck)
Spinnaker sheet and guy (length 8 m, diameter 3 or 4 mm)
Spinnaker halyard (length 9 m, diameter 3 or 4 mm)
Spinnaker crane
5 mini blocks
4 stainless steel dead eyes
1 clam cleat
1 cam cleat
Net with 4 HA328 hooks, or chute with sock
Plastic clip to hold halyard to gunwale

Personally I prefer a net to a chute because it is much kinder to the spinnaker—but a chute is a little easier to use. If you do fit one, put it on the port side of the forestay since this makes life easier on an Olympic course. (However, many chutes are designed to be fitted to starboard!)
I also prefer a support rod for the spinnaker boom rather than a rope downhaul. It is far easier for the crew to get up and down, and easier when gybing. The rod holds the boom rigid and so makes control of the spinnaker easier. The rod is attached to the boom by a universal joint.

The spinnaker sheet and guy is one continuous rope, tensioned by a pulley and a short length of rope near the stern. The crew can adjust the sheet and guy simultaneously with this system. In heavy winds, cleats can be useful with young crews.

The spinnaker halyard passes through a crane fixed on top of the mast. This keeps it clear of the other rigging. The halyard goes down to a mini block mounted low on the storage bulkhead, then back to a cam cleat mounted under the thwart. This makes it handy for the helmsman to grab when raising or lowering the spinnaker.

The diagrams on the opposite page illustrate the system, and Figure 6.4 shows the gear in action. Raising, setting, gybing and lowering the spinnaker are discussed in Chapter 14.

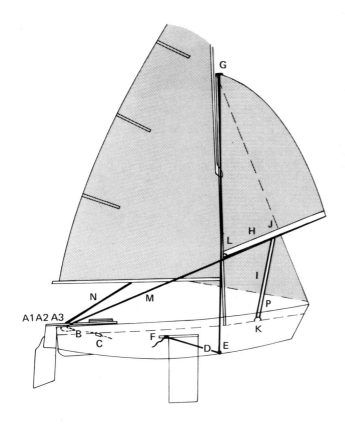

A1, A3 mini blocks fixed to gunwale
A2 mini block fixed to transom
B mini block with rope tail
C clam cleat to hold rope tail
D spinnaker halyard
E mini block to take spinnaker halyard,
   set low on bulkhead
F cam cleat to hold spinnaker halyard
G crane for spinnaker halyard
H spinnaker boom
I spinnaker boom support rod
J universal joint
K spinnaker boom bracket on foredeck.
   Support rod clips onto this
L spinnaker boom bracket on front of
   mast
M guy
N sheet (continuous with guy)
O net, with elastic front and aft edges
P clip to keep halyard clear of jib
   when spinnaker not in use

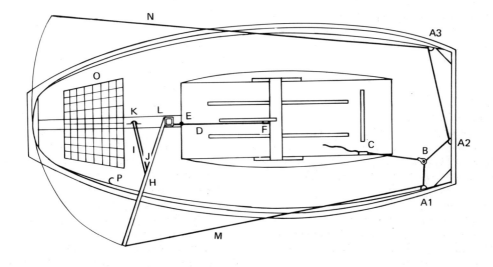

4.10

5 Launching

With practice, you will find you can get afloat quickly and easily in most conditions.

How you launch depends on the wind direction relative to the shore. However, a few points always apply:

- Rig the boat on the shore.

- Keep the boat pointing into the wind at all times. Let the sails flap freely—make sure the sheets are slack.

- The hull is easily damaged. Keep it off the ground at all costs.

Launching with the wind along the shore

This is the easiest wind direction to launch in (Fig. 5.1).

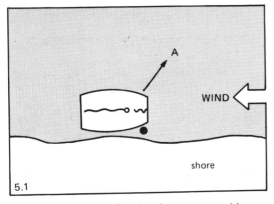

5.1

1 Get your boat rigged, but leave your rudder blade up and don't put the centreboard in yet.

2 Put the boat in the water, keeping it pointing into the wind. The helmsman holds the boat, standing in the water near the bow.

3 See that your trolley is left safely—remember the tide!

4 The crew climbs aboard, puts in the centreboard and pushes down the rudder until they both just clear the bottom.

5 The helmsman makes sure that the mainsheet is running free and the tiller extension points towards him.

6 The helmsman turns the boat slightly away from the shore, pushes it forward and steps in on the windward side. Aim to sail in direction A. Pull in the sails, encouraging the boat to move forward slowly. *Don't* try to go too fast with the rudder blade up—you may snap it.

7 As soon as the water is deep enough, let out the sails (keeping the boat in direction A) and push the centreboard and rudder right down.

Launching with an offshore wind

Follow *exactly* the same method as for launching with the wind along the shore. DO NOT try to turn the boat round and sail straight out—it will sail away before you have time to jump in! Aim to get off in direction B (Fig. 5.2).

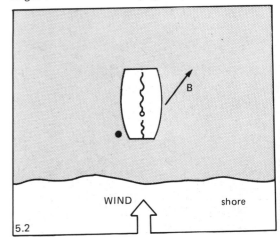

5.2

Launching with an onshore wind

This is the most difficult wind direction for launching, because the wind tends to push you back on shore (Fig. 5.3).

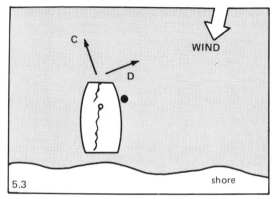

5.3   shore

Put the boat in the water, following the first five steps described above. You will have to beat to get away from the shore, so choose which tack you are going to take. In the diagram, C is better than D because the wind is coming more from the right and C will take you offshore faster.

The helmsman gives the boat a good push and steps aboard (Fig. 5.4). Pull in the sails quickly and hike out. Gradually push the centreboard down as you 'crab' offshore. Finally, when you're well out, stop and lower the rudder blade fully.

5.4

Launching in very shallow water

Wade out, towing the boat, until the water is at least up to your knees (deeper if the wind is onshore).

Launching in waves—onshore wind

Rig the boat at the water's edge with the bow into the wind. Decide which tack you're going on. The helmsman stands on the side that will be to windward, with the tiller extension out to this side. The helmsman holds the mainsheet in his front hand while the crew stands on the opposite (leeward) side of the boat. Watch for a lull in the waves—it will come, but you may have to wait a few minutes. Run forward with the boat, and as the water gets deep push the boat forward. The crew rolls into the boat a second or two before the helmsman hauls himself on board. Hike out, and try to sail as fast as possible. If the boat gets washed back in, jump out to *windward* at the last moment. Try not to get between the boat and the shore—a big wave may push the boat into you and do you a lot of damage. If you do get trapped like this, keep your back to the boat or it may hit your knees 'wrong way on' and break your leg. But if it's that rough, maybe you should stay ashore!

Launching from a jetty

Be sure to launch your boat on the leeward side of the jetty! (Fig. 5.5)

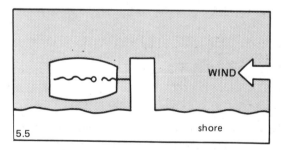

5.5   shore

To get aboard, pull the boat in until it is nearly sideways to the jetty, bow pointing to open water. The helmsman steps in onto the thwart, and pushes down the rudder blade and the centreboard. The crew meanwhile unties the painter and then steps aboard, giving the boat a push off. Pull in the jib and mainsheet and sail off.

19

6 Reaching

Reaching is fun! It's the fastest point of sailing and the easiest to control.

What is reaching?

The boats in Fig. 6.1 are reaching. Their courses are roughly at right angles to the wind.

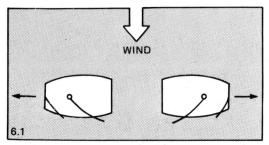

6.1

Adjusting the sails

The secret of reaching is sail trim (Fig. 6.2). Keeping a straight course, let the sails out until they begin to flap at the front (just behind the mast or forestay). Then pull in the sails until they just stop flapping.

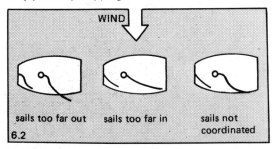

sails too far out   sails too far in   sails not coordinated

6.2

The wind changes in direction every few seconds, so the sails must be trimmed constantly. Keep the sheets in your hands all the time, and 'play' them in and out.

If the sails flap, they're too far out. If the boat heels over and slows down, the sails are too far in. When the sails are about right, they will be roughly in line with the burgee and with each other.

Every time you change course, you must adjust the sheets—pull them in further if you change course closer to the wind, let them out if you change course away from the wind.

Steering

Try to keep a reasonably straight course: each time you alter course, you will have to adjust the sails. If there is a strong 'pull' on the tiller extension, it's usually because the boat is heeling over too much. Hike out to bring the boat level; the pull will disappear and you can steer easily.

Trim

Both fore-and-aft and sideways movements of your bodies affect the boat's trim.

Normally, the helmsman and crew sit so that their centre of gravity (the midpoint of their combined weights) is on the centreline of the thwart. This presents the best hull shape to the water. Move forwards in light winds to reduce the amount of hull skin in the water (and so reduce skin friction). Move aft in strong winds to lift the bow and help the boat to plane.

Move your weight to keep the boat absolutely upright. This will make steering much easier—if the boat heels, the asymmetric hull shape is forced to turn to one side.

Centreboard

Have the centreboard half up, to reduce drag and make the boat easier to handle. If it slips down, tighten the elastic shockcord. If you want to change course closer to the wind, push the centreboard down slightly; pull it up if you change course away from the wind.

Fig. 6.3 shows good reaching technique. The helmsman and crew are using their weight to keep the boat absolutely level. The crew's attention is on the front part of the jib (as well as where they're going!) and he continually adjusts the jibsheet. The helmsman continually adjusts the mainsheet; because the boat is level, he can steer gently and easily. The kicking strap (vang) is tight, but the other controls are loose. The mainsail has a good curve in it for maximum power.

Gusts

Look over your shoulder occasionally to see if a gust is coming. The water looks dark as a gust travels over it.

When the gust hits, hike out further. If the boat still heels over, let the sheets out until the boat comes level. Don't forget to pull the sheets back in again as the gust passes, or the boat will heel over on top of you.

Don't let the gust turn the boat round into the wind. Be firm with the tiller and keep the boat going in the direction *you* want.

Sail controls

The mainsail should be set so there is a good curve or belly in the sail.

The kicking strap (vang) should be 'normal' (see page 15).

The downhaul should be loose. Let the rope off until creases appear along the front edge of the sail. Then pull in the rope until the creases just disappear. The maximum belly should come back to the middle of the sail.

The sail outhaul should be loose. You should be able to get your fist between the foot of the sail and the middle of the boom.

In stronger winds, all three sail controls should be tighter. In light winds, they should be looser.

Going faster

If you want to win races, it's essential to be able to reach fast. Here are some points to watch and ideas to try.

- Keep the boat absolutely upright.

- Adjust the sheets all the time.

- Use your body weight. Hike out as far as you can. Move back in gusts, forward in lulls. If the boat heels, try to bring it upright with your weight before letting out the sheets.

- Steer a straight course. Don't weave about—the rudder acts as a brake each time you use it.

- In a strong gust, alter course away from the wind, easing the sheets. Get back on course when the gust has passed.

- Turn away from the wind each time a wave picks up the boat. Try to surf on each wave.

- Try fixing a 'telltale' on your jib about 60 cm up from the foot and about 15 cm back from the forestay (see page 14). When the sail is properly adjusted, the wool should stream back on both sides of the sail. If the jib is too far in, the leeward telltale will collapse; too far out, and the windward one will collapse.

- Use the spinnaker whenever possible (the spinnaker is discussed on pages 48-55).

REACHING IN LIGHT WINDS

Reaching in light winds needs patience. Try to keep still—if the boat rocks about the wind is 'shaken' out of the sails.

Trim

Sit right forward to lift the stern of the boat clear of the water. This cuts down the wetted area of the hull and hence the friction between the hull and the water.

Heel the boat to leeward. This cuts down further on the wetted area of the hull and keeps the sails in the correct shape. In very light winds the helmsman can take the weight of the boom on his shoulder while sitting to leeward. This 'opens' the leech and reduces drag.

Gusts

Change course away from the wind and try to stay with the gust as long as possible. At the same time hike out to bring the boat upright: this fans the boat forward. Then get back on or above your course and wait for the next gust.

Sail controls

The downhaul and outhaul should be loose. The kicking strap should be loosened completely in very light airs. The jib halyard should be no tighter than is needed to keep the jib luff just straight between the hanks. If the spinnaker is not filling, try pulling the guy and spinnaker boom towards you. If the spinnaker still doesn't fill, take it down.

Steering

Hold the tiller extension gently and try to alter course as little as possible. If the boat is stopped, try using your weight to bring the boat gently upright, at the same time slowly pulling in the mainsheet—but only *once* if you're racing!

Burgee

In light winds, it's important to keep an eye on your burgee and the ripples on the water to spot changes in wind direction. Your burgee should be balanced or it will turn as the boat heels.

REACHING IN STRONG WINDS

Reaching in a good breeze is the ultimate in Mirror sailing, particularly if you're flying a spinnaker (Fig. 6.4). It's surprising how fast the boat can go, especially down waves. At these high speeds the helmsman and crew must act quickly and firmly.

6.4

Adjusting the sails

Hike out hard. Pull the mainsail in as far as you can while keeping the boat level. If you are flying a spinnaker and need to turn away from the wind to keep control, do so. You can always get back on course in a lull, or take the spinnaker down before approaching the buoy.

Steering

Keep a good grip on the tiller extension. If the boat heels, turn into the wind slightly and let the sails out a little. By adjusting the mainsheet, spinnaker sheet and tiller you can keep the boat upright and go really fast. You will need to make an adjustment at least every couple of seconds.

Try to steer down waves as much as possible. As a wave picks up the boat, turn away from the wind and surf down the wave.

Trim

Both helmsman and crew should hike nearer the stern; this lets the bow of the boat come up and skim over the water—this is *planing*.

Gusts

Don't let a gust slew the boat round into the wind. If you do, the quick turn will capsize you. As the gust hits, let the sails out slightly and turn 10° to 20° away from the wind. This lets the boat 'ride with the punch'. Try to keep breathing, despite the spray!

If the boat rolls, pull the sails in and use your weight to 'dampen' the roll. Check that the centreboard is half down.

In a real squall, keep on a reach with most of the sails flapping. If you are caught with the spinnaker up, turn onto a run. Get the spinnaker down before you come back onto a reach.

Sail controls

In strong winds, all sail controls should be bar tight. There is no chance of adjusting them as you sail round the course.

1 The crew is dreaming—he needs to concentrate on the jib, which is flapping. He should pull in the jibsheet until the sail just stops flapping, and the telltales stream back on both sides of the sail.

2 Both main and jib are pulled in too far—note the wind direction shown by the burgee. Both sails should be let out until they are almost in line with the burgee, and until they nearly begin to flap.

REACHING—SOME COMMON MISTAKES

3 The mainsail and jib should be parallel. Here, the jib is much too far in and is spoiling the boat's performance.

4 Both helmsman and crew are sitting too far back. The stern is dragging in the water—notice the wave this has caused behind the boat. Only sit this far back when the boat is planing.

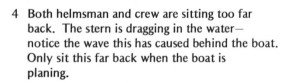

7 Beating

Beating in a Mirror, particularly in a blow, is one of the most satisfying parts of sailing. You are, literally, beating the wind which is trying to push you back.

What is beating?

A boat cannot sail straight from A to B (Fig. 7.1). The sail will flap, and the boat will be blown backwards. The only way is to beat—to sail a zigzag course at an angle of about 45° to the wind.

Steering

To beat, pull in the mainsheet and jibsheet firmly, hike out, and steer as close to the wind as you can (Fig. 7.3). The course is a compromise: if you steer too close to the wind you slow down, even though you are pointing closer to B. If you steer too far from the wind, you go faster, but are pointing well away from B (Fig. 7.2).

The simplest check on your course is to watch the front of the jib. Turn towards the wind until the jib begins to flap, then turn back until it just stops flapping. You are now on course. Repeat this every few seconds—both to check your course, and because the wind constantly changes its direction. If you have telltales on the jib, they should be streaming on both sides of the sail. If the windward one drops, turn away from the wind; if the leeward one drops turn towards the wind.

At points X and Y the boat tacks through about 90°. Tacking is discussed on page 30.

Adjusting the sails

When beating in medium or light winds there is no need to adjust the sheets. Keep them pulled in, and concentrate on using the tiller to keep the boat at the proper angle to the wind. Even though the jibsheet is cleated, the crew should keep the loose part in his hand so he can release it in a gust.

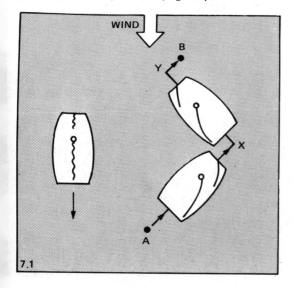

7.1

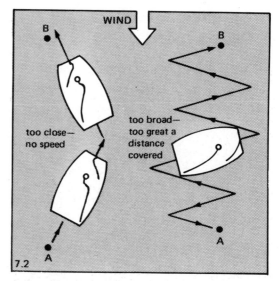

7.2

The tension of the sheets is important. In medium winds, pull in the mainsheet firmly. In light and in very strong winds, you will need to let the mainsheet out a little.

When the jib is sheeted to the gunwale the crew pulls the jibsheet tight except in very light winds. If inboard sheeting is used the crew pulls in the jib tight, then releases about 5 cm. The jib may 'backwind' the mainsail—i.e. push air onto the leeward side of the mainsail: watch the front of the mainsail which will appear to flap. If this happens, ease the jibsheet or try lowering the jib tack to open the slot between jib leech and mainsail. Another remedy is to move the fairleads aft.

Trim

In flat water sit forward with the centre of gravity of helmsman and crew (the midpoint of your combined weights) on a line one-third of the way back from the front edge of the thwart.

In rough seas, the helmsman sits as if planing —his aft leg against the rear bulkhead—while the crew sits back level with the thwart.

The boat must always be sailed absolutely upright, except in the lightest of airs when it should be heeled to leeward.

Centreboard

The centreboard should be pushed right down when beating.

Gusts

The water looks dark as a gust travels over it. As the gust hits you, hike out hard and turn into the wind a few degrees. If the boat still heels, let the mainsail out a little. When the boat has picked up speed, pull the sail in again. When the gust has passed, move your weight inboard and adjust your course as necessary.

Windshifts

The wind constantly alters in direction. However, some changes are larger and/or last longer. These are windshifts, and it is vital you spot them and react to them when racing. Windshifts are discussed on page 62.

Sail controls

The sail should be set flatter than when reaching or running.

The kicking strap (vang) should be 'normal' (see page 15) or, in strong winds, tighter than 'normal'.

The downhaul should be tight enough to keep the greatest camber in the mainsail two-fifths of the way back from the mast. There should be no horizontal creases in the front of the mainsail.

The stronger the wind, the more tension you need on the outhaul: if you are overpowered, pull the outhaul tighter. In choppy water ease the outhaul off slightly to put more curve in the bottom of the sail—this provides more power to get over the waves. You will not then be able to steer so close to the wind, but the extra speed more than compensates for the extra distance sailed. Try to get a compromise setting according to wind strength and wave conditions. It is a good idea to mark the settings on the boom alongside the outhaul slide, so that you can find the right setting more easily.

Going faster

Most races start with a beat and it's essential to get to the first mark well up in the fleet. Here are some points to watch and some ideas to try:

- Keep the boat absolutely upright.

- Keep the mainsheet pulled in tight except in very light and very strong winds.

- Hike as hard as you can. Only let the mainsail out as a last resort.

- Watch the front of the jib like a hawk. Keep altering course so the jib just doesn't flap (so the telltales stream on both sides).

- Don't slam the bow into waves.

- Watch out for windshifts.

- Keep a good lookout for other boats.

BEATING IN LIGHT WINDS

Aim for speed rather than steering very close to the wind. Keep an eye on the water and on your burgee to spot windshifts.

Adjusting the sails

Pull in the mainsheet gently so the boom is over the quarter. The jibsheet should also be a little looser than normal. Most people make the mistake of pointing the boat too close to the wind in very light airs, so lay off and aim for speed. When a gust comes, let the mainsheet out a little; as the boat gathers speed, pull the mainsheet back in —but not too tight.

Steering

Hold the tiller extension gently. Watch the front of the jib and steer as close to the wind as you can without the jib flapping. You will find you need to alter course every few seconds to keep 'on the wind'.

Trim

Sit forward in flat water until the bow is buried about 5 cm and heel the boat to leeward. Both actions cut down the wetted area of the hull.

Sail controls

Set the kicking strap just tight enough to stop the boom lifting. It shouldn't pull it down. If you have telltales at the batten pockets, they should all stream horizontally (with sufficient wind). If the middle batten telltale doesn't stream, then there is too much tension on the leech of the main —either the mainsheet or kicking strap is too tight.

The downhaul should be fairly slack. Wrinkles up the luff in *very* light winds are OK.

The sail outhaul should be fairly tight to flatten the sail in very light winds.

BEATING IN STRONG WINDS

In these conditions both the wind and the waves tend to stop the boat. You must not let this happen because you can only steer when the boat is moving—so speed through the waves is your main aim.

Adjusting the sails

Try to beat with the mainsheet pulled in as tight as possible. This bends the gaff and mast, reducing the curve in the mainsail. To keep the boat level, you will have to point close to the wind—the front part of the jib and main will flutter most of the time.

In very strong winds the boat may stop if you use this technique. Ease the mainsheet a little and as soon as the bow is pushed away from the wind

ease the jib a little and 'reach' to windward. As speed is increased point higher, pulling in the main and jib sheets.

Steering over waves

Try to steer so the boat has an easy passage over the waves. As the bow goes up a wave, push the tiller away a little. Pull the tiller as the bow reaches the crest, and turn away down the back of the wave. Repeat this for each wave—you will find you're moving the tiller all the time. Keep hiking as hard as you can.

Centreboard

In very strong winds, pull the centreboard up 10 to 20 cm. This lets the boat slide sideways and 'ride with the punch'.

Hiking

Your body weight provides the power to get to windward. The more you hike, the faster you go. Adjust the toestraps so you're comfortable. It's easier to lever yourselves back into the boat if the toestraps are low in the cockpit; but they should be high enough so you can get your feet under them quickly.

Trim

In large waves, the helmsman moves back between the thwart and aft buoyancy compartment, and the crew sits level with the middle of the thwart; this lets the bow ride over the waves more easily. Try leaning towards the stern as the boat goes up a wave, and forwards as it goes down.

Gusts

Let the sheets out as much as is necessary to keep the boat upright and moving.

Sail controls

The kicking strap, downhaul and outhaul should all be bar tight.

1 Mirrors, like all dinghies, sail fastest when dead upright. Both helmsman and crew seem to have forgotten to hike.

BEATING—SOME COMMON MISTAKES

3 The helmsman is pointing too close to the wind —or 'pinching'. Both he and the crew are sitting too far back.

2 The main halyard is too loose—this is causing the horrible creases in the mainsail. The jib halyard could also do with tightening: note the sagging of the jib luff between the hanks. Rigging like this brings tears to every sailmaker's eyes.

4 The boat is pointing too far from the wind (note the direction of the burgee). The helmsman may be doing this to 'support' the crew, who is still hiking despite a lull in the wind.

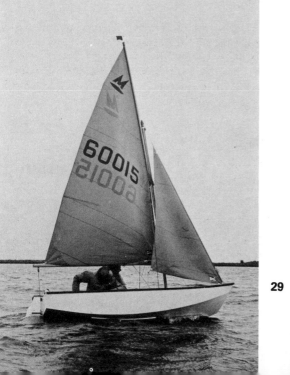

8 Tacking

What is tacking?

The boat in Fig. 8.1 is beating with the sails on the port side (a). The boat turns into the wind (b), and keeps turning until it is beating with the sails on the starboard side (c). The turn is called a tack.

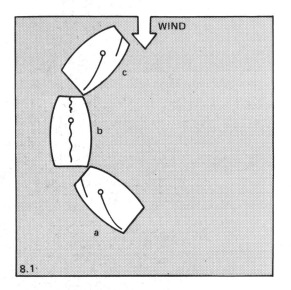

WIND

8.1

Six steps to a good tack—helmsman

1 *Get some speed*. Hike extra hard to get the boat moving as fast as possible. You will need this speed to turn 'through' the wind and waves. Warn the crew that you're going to tack ('ready about' is the traditional phrase). Let the boat heel a little to leeward (Fig. 8.2 opposite).

2 *Turn*. Still hiking, and with the sheets still pulled in, push the tiller away from you (Fig. 8.3). Push gently at first, then a little harder. Shout 'lee oh' to the crew. Keep the tiller pushed over until step 5.

3 *Change hands*. Clamp the mainsheet under the thumb of the hand holding the tiller extension. You now have both sheet and extension in your 'back' hand. Grab the tiller extension with your 'front' hand. Lift your 'back' hand off the extension, holding the sheet. In this way you change hands on the sheet and tiller without letting go of either (Fig. 8.4). Swivel the tiller extension round forwards.

4 *Cross the boat*. As the boom comes over, dive across the boat facing aft, ducking as you go under the boom! Keep the boat turning as you do so. (Fig. 8.5)

5 *Straighten up*. As you land on the new side, begin to straighten up. Don't let the boat spin round too far (onto a reach)—you are trying to get to windward. You should turn through about 90°—note the angle in the wake in Fig. 8.6.

6 *Go*. Pull in the sheet and hike out on the new side (Fig. 8.7).

The crew's job is described on p. 32.

Roll tacking

In lighter winds, roll tacking can help you tack faster. Plenty of practice is needed to reach perfection as the combined weight of helmsman and crew must move in harmony.

Lean the boat to leeward just before you start to tack, with the mainsheet eased out a few centimetres. As you start to turn, bring the boat upright and pull the mainsheet in. This makes the sails fan the wind, pushing the boat forwards.

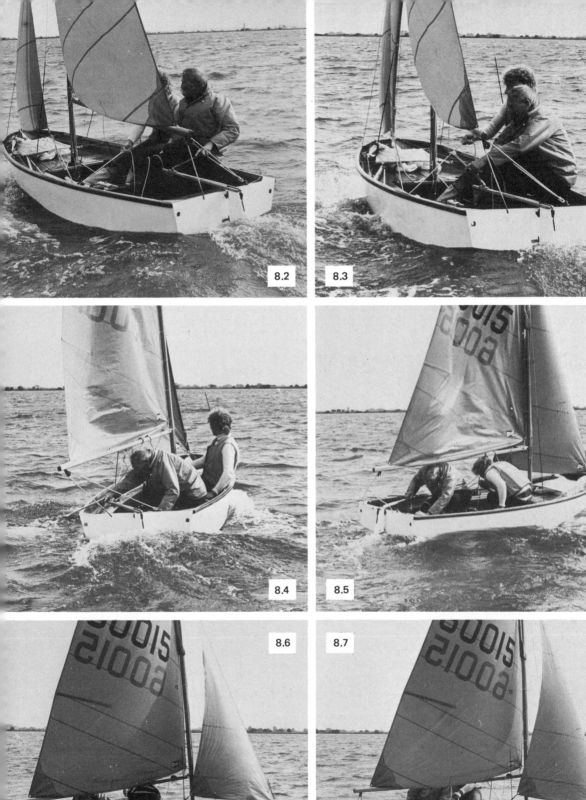

8.2

8.3

8.4

8.5

8.6

8.7

8.8

As the turn continues, stay on the 'old' side. The boat will start to roll on top of you. Release the mainsheet a few centimetres. When the gunwale is almost awash the helmsman and crew move gently to the 'new' windward side. Pull in the mainsheet as the boat comes upright, fanning the boat forward a second time.

Six steps to a good tack—crew

1 *Get some speed.* Hike hard to get the boat moving. Uncleat the jibsheet, but hold it in your aft hand and keep it pulled in until step 5.

2 *Grab the new jibsheet.* Take the opposite jibsheet in your front hand.

3 *Keep hiking.* Stay on the windward side as the helmsman starts to turn (Fig. 8.8).

4 *Change sides.* As the helmsman lands on the 'new' side, start to cross the boat. Face aft, take the new jibsheet with you but keep the old jibsheet pulled tight. This 'backing' of the jib helps spin the boat (Fig. 8.9).

5 *Pull the jib across.* As you land on the new side pay out the old jibsheet and pull in the new one (Fig. 8.10).

6 *Go.* Hike out and cleat the jibsheet. Encourage your helmsman to drive the boat faster (Fig. 8.11).

8.9

8.10

8.11

1 Only back the jib for a moment. If you wait too long the boat is blown round too far, and may even capsize. Either way, your helmsman may gently point out your error!

2 The tack is completed, but the helmsman let go of the mainsheet. Now he has to pull it all in again, just when he should be accelerating after the tack.

TACKING—SOME COMMON MISTAKES

3 Straightening up too early leaves the boat pointing straight into the wind. This may also happen if you tack without building up enough speed.

4 Forgetting to straighten up brings the boat round too far—onto a reach in this case. This time, the crew may take the opportunity to mention the mistake!

9 Running

What is running?

Both boats in Fig. 9.1 are running—i.e. they are sailing with the wind directly behind.

Adjusting the sails

In medium and light winds the mainsheet should be as far out as possible while the crew holds the jib sheet out on the opposite side, preferably with a jibstick. This is called goosewinging.

In strong winds the helmsman and crew must counterbalance any rolling immediately by moving their weight or by pulling in the mainsheet a little.

Trim

In light to medium winds sit forward, but slide back to dig the stern into overtaking waves, sliding forward again when the stern is lifted. Heel the boat to windward to reduce rudder drag as well as to make the boat more responsive to tiller movement.

The boat is least likely to roll if the helmsman and crew sit on opposite sides of the boat. Personally I prefer to sit to leeward while my crew sits to windward.

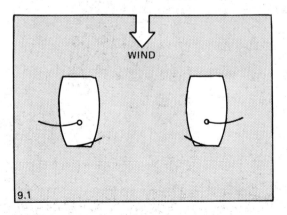

Steering

Avoid violent turns—the boat is travelling fast and 'centrifugal' force may capsize you. Aim to turn smoothly and slowly.

It is vital to avoid an unexpected gybe (gybing is discussed on page 38). Watch the burgee carefully and avoid turning so that the wind is blowing from the same side as the boom (Fig. 9.2). This is

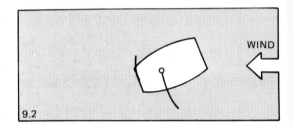

'running by the lee'—the wind is able to get behind the boom and flip it across. If you find yourself in this position, turn quickly so the wind blows dead behind the boat.

Centreboard

Pull the centreboard up so that only a few centimetres are in the water. In very strong winds, leave the centreboard at least half down to dampen rolling. Never have the centreboard right down when running. Never take the centreboard out when running—this creates too much turbulence in the centreboard box.

Gusts

Keep going, even in strong gusts. Don't let the gust turn the boat round into the wind—keep a straight course. If the boat rolls, pull in the mainsheet. If the boat heels away from you, let the mainsheet out. If it heels towards you, pull the mainsheet in.

Sail controls

The kicking strap (vang) should be 'normal' (page 15) except in light winds when it should be slacker than normal.

The downhaul should be loose; aim for a lot of curve in the sail. The outhaul should be fairly tight.

Going faster

You can often gain a good number of places on a run, particularly if you are towards the back of the fleet and the wind comes up. Those in front are at your mercy because you can blanket them from the wind. Here are some points to watch and ideas to try:

- Let the mainsheet out as far as possible.

- If you aren't using a spinnaker, use a jibstick to hold the jib out on the opposite side to the mainsail.

- Make sure you have the centreboard well up.

- Fly the spinnaker (using a spinnaker is discussed on pages 48-55).

- Heel the boat to windward until the 'pull' on the tiller stops. You can now steer the boat by heel—if you heel it towards you the boat will turn away from you and vice versa.

- When a gust comes, run straight down wind with it. Try to stay with the gust as long as possible. If you see a gust to one side of the course, sail over to it and then ride it.

- Try to surf on waves as much as you can. Pull the mainsheet in a little as the boat accelerates down each wave.

RUNNING IN LIGHT WINDS

Trim

Both helmsman and crew should be sitting in front of the thwart on opposite sides of the boat. One should hold the boom out while the other goose-wings the jib. Only a few centimetres of centreboard need be in the water. If there is enough wind to fill the sails, heel the boat to windward. In *very* light winds, heel the boat to leeward.

Steering

Use the tiller as little as possible. Try to balance the boat to windward so that the boat sails straight without the helmsman holding the tiller. Try to keep absolutely still.

Sail controls

The kicking strap should be just firm enough to prevent the boom lifting. This allows the gaff to straighten and puts more curve into the sail. The downhaul should be loose, but the outhaul should be fairly tight.

RUNNING IN STRONG WINDS

Trim

The centre of gravity of helmsman and crew should be at least 20 cm behind the aft edge of the thwart. Move back still further if there is a risk of burying the bow into the wave ahead. A spinnaker stabilizes the boat, once it is up and filled; the boat need not be heeled to windward as much when flying a spinnaker.

Steering

Be prepared to make corrections immediately if a wave pushes the boat off course. It is essential that the rudder blade is near vertical to reduce leverage on the tiller (see page 14 for advice on replacing the elastic rudder downhaul).

Try to sail down the waves. As a wave comes up behind, turn away from the wind and surf on the wave. Be very careful not to turn so far that you gybe.

Sail controls

All controls should be bar tight. A jibstick is essential to enable the crew to move further aft.

Centreboard

Keep the centreboard half down; this helps prevent rolling.

1 Heel the boat slightly to windward, not to leeward. The crew should move to windward to balance the helmsman.

2 In medium or light winds, sit forward. Note the turbulence caused by the stern digging into the water.

RUNNING—SOME COMMON MISTAKES

3 The jib is doing nothing. Goosewinging it will bring it out from behind the mainsail into some 'clean' air.

4 The kicking strap should be tightened to stop the boom lifting skywards.

10 Gybing

What is gybing?

In Fig. 10.1, boat (a) is running with the mainsail on the starboard side. The helmsman turns through a small angle (b). The wind forces the mainsail out to the port side of the boat (c). The turn is called a *gybe*.

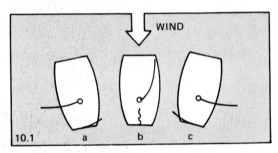

Why is gybing difficult?

Gybing is the hardest sailing manoeuvre. Unlike tacking, the wind pushes on the sail throughout the turn. The boat is moving at high speed, so is very sensitive to tiller movements. A miscalculation results in the boat rolling—with the sails 'edge on' there's not much to dampen the roll and you tend to take an involuntary dip.

Decide when you want to gybe, and then do it! The best moment is when the boat is moving fast down a wave—since you're travelling away from the wind, the 'push' on the sail is lessened.

Gybing with a spinnaker is described on p. 52.

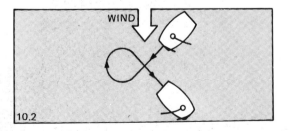

Six steps to a good gybe—helmsman

1 *Get ready*. Warn the crew (shout 'stand by to gybe') and check that he has pushed down the centreboard. Turn the boat until the wind is almost directly behind (Fig. 10.3).

2 *Pull in the mainsheet*. Pull in an arm's length of mainsheet and clamp it in your tiller hand. Heel the boat to windward—if you let it heel to leeward, you can't turn (Fig. 10.4).

3 *Turn*. Firmly but slowly, pull the tiller towards you (Fig. 10.5). Shout 'gybe oh' to your crew.

4 *Cross the boat*. As the boom comes over, cross the boat facing aft. Don't forget to duck! As you move across, keep the mainsheet in your tiller hand (Fig. 10.6).

5 *Steer*. As you land on the new side, pull the tiller towards you. This stops the boat turning through too large an angle. Let the mainsheet slide through your fingers so the boom can go right out (Fig. 10.7).

6 *Change hands*. Grab the tiller extension with your aft hand, keeping the mainsheet in your front hand (Fig. 10.8). If the boat rolls, pull in the mainsheet for a few seconds and move inboard as necessary.

As you gain confidence, try changing hands on the mainsheet and tiller extension as you are midway through the gybe.

Gybing in very strong winds

In very strong winds a capsize may be inevitable. If you can't pull the mainsheet in on the run, it's better to wear round. This involves turning through 360° as shown in Fig. 10.2. Do this with the centreboard right down. Pull in the mainsheet and spin the boat around fast.

10.3

10.4

10.5

10.6

10.7

10.8

Six steps to a good gybe—crew

1 *Lower the centreboard fully.* If you forget to do this you'll be trapped on the wrong side of the centreboard and will probably capsize.

2 *Uncleat the jibsheet.* The jib is best left flapping during the gybe, so uncleat the jibsheet and let it go.

3 *Grab the new jibsheet.* Take the opposite jibsheet in your aft hand so you're ready to adjust the sail after the gybe.

4 *Pull the kicking strap.* As the boom starts to move, use your forward hand to pull it across by the kicking strap (Fig. 10.9).

5 *Cross the boat.* The wind will suddenly get behind the mainsail and flip the boom across. As it does so, duck underneath and cross the boat.

6 *Trim the jib.* Pull in the new jibsheet as much as is needed to fill the jib. Use your weight to stabilize the boat.

HOW NOT TO GYBE

In the sequence of photographs opposite, everything goes wrong:

In Fig. 10.10 the crew has forgotten to push down the centreboard. The helmsman turns viciously (Fig. 10.11) without pulling in any mainsheet.

Too late, the crew realizes he's trapped to leeward by the centreboard (Fig. 10.12). The helmsman has straightened up too late—the boat has spun round almost onto a reach.

Fig. 10.13 shows the inevitable result. The crew hasn't helped by pulling in the new jibsheet; the jib is pulling the boat over even quicker. But perhaps he's using the sheet as a lifeline!

(This sequence of photos is continued on page 43.)

10.9

10.10

10.11

10.12

10.13

11 Capsizing

Everyone capsizes. Indeed, if you don't capsize sometimes, you're probably not really trying.

Never leave the boat (to swim for the shore, for example). The hull will support you almost indefinitely—it has enough buoyancy inside to float even if the hull is punctured—and is more easily spotted than a swimmer.

The boat will tip one of two ways: to leeward, or to windward (which is less pleasant).

Avoiding a capsize to leeward

- Watch for gusts.

- Keep the sheets in your hands at all times. Let them out if a gust strikes.

- Hike in strong winds.

- On a reach or run, don't let the boat turn fast into the wind.

- In very strong winds, avoid pulling the spinnaker up and down on a reach. Instead, turn onto a run while you are raising or lowering it.

- If a gust hits you on a spinnaker reach, pull the spinnaker to windward to make it flap and lose power.

Avoiding a capsize to windward

- Be ready to move your weight inboard in lulls.

- Pull in the sheets rapidly if the boat rolls to windward.

- On a reach or run, avoid turning fast away from the wind.

- When running under spinnaker, pull it to leeward as the boat rolls to windward.

Righting the boat

When the inevitable happens, try to turn around so that you are facing 'uphill'. One of you may be able to scramble over the gunwale onto the centreboard and pull the boat upright again, diving into the cockpit at the last minute. If you both fall in, then follow the procedure below:

1 The crew swims to the stern, while the helmsman swims around the stern of the boat to the centreboard, holding the mainsheet as a lifeline (Fig. 11.1).

2 The helmsman holds the centreboard, stopping the boat turning upside down; the crew pushes the centreboard right down and throws a jibsheet over the top of the hull to the helmsman. The crew then lies in the water on the leeward side of the boat.

3 The helmsman pulls himself onto the centreboard, using the jibsheet to help him (Fig. 11.2).

4 As the boat comes upright, the crew is scooped on board (Figs. 11.3, 11.4).

5 If the helmsman is quick, he can also get aboard as the boat comes upright. If not, the crew can pull him in over the stern (Fig. 11.5).

Tidy the gear inside the cockpit and get sailing as soon as possible. There should be very little water in the cockpit: if there is, the self bailer will soon get rid of it.

The capsize illustrated on this page was made worse because the rudder came adrift. Make sure the rudder retaining clip is adjusted properly before you go afloat.

If the boat turns completely upside down, the helmsman should climb on top; he can then pull the boat onto its side, using the centreboard as a lever (make sure you bring the mast up to leeward

11.1

11.2

11.3

11.4

of the hull). Then right the boat as described above.

Some boats have a stirrup fixed through a hole in the stern to help you climb onto the upturned hull, or to climb back into the righted boat.

In shallow water, don't let the boat turn upside down or the gaff may snap.

If the gaff gets stuck in mud, stand on the centreboard close to the hull and gently bounce up and down to free it.

11.5

12 Landing

The way you land will depend on the direction of the wind relative to the shore. Landing badly can do a good deal of damage to the boat (and even to yourselves); always remember, for instance, to push up your self bailer and to undo your rudder downhaul (if you have one) in good time.

Landing with the wind along the shore

This is the easiest wind direction for landing.

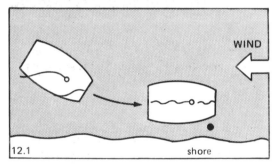

12.1   shore

1 Sail slowly towards the shore as shown in Fig. 12.1. Control the boat's speed with the sheets, letting them out as you approach to slow the boat down.

2 At the last minute, take out the centreboard and turn into the wind.

3 One of you steps into the water on the shore side of the boat, holding it as near the bow as possible.

4 Make sure the sheets are free.

5 Pull down the sails.

Landing with an offshore wind (Fig. 12.2)

Beat in towards the shore. On the approach leg A, control the speed with the sheets. At the last moment, take out the centreboard, and turn the

boat into the wind. The crew steps into the water as near the bow as possible; then proceed as above.

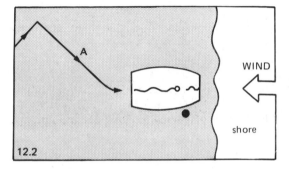

12.2

Landing with an onshore wind (Fig. 12.3)

This is the most difficult direction for landing because the wind is pushing you onshore fast. Unless the waves are very big, land as follows:

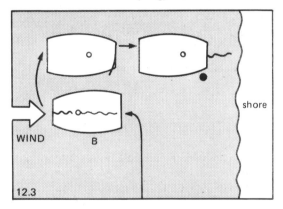

12.3

1 Sail parallel to the shore, about 50 metres out.

2 Turn into the wind (B) and lower the mainsail.

3 Point the boat towards the shore and let it drift in. Control the speed with the jib. If you are still going too fast, trail a leg in the water as a brake.

12.4

4 At the last minute, take out the centreboard (Fig. 12.4). The crew steps into the water and holds the boat.

Landing in very shallow water

Come in slowly. Lift up the rudder blade in good time and step into the water early.

Landing in big waves and an onshore wind

The method described above won't work in very large waves, because of the danger of one rolling the boat over. Use the following technique instead.

1 While well offshore, undo the rudder downhaul and hold it in your tiller hand. The rudder blade will come up when it hits the beach. Don't pull up the blade—you need all the control you can get. Pull the centreboard three-quarters up.

2 As you get near the beach, choose the smallest wave you can find and surf full speed on it towards the beach. Keep the bow pointing straight at the shore. Sit one on either side of the boat, well back to let the bow ride up the

beach. As the boat grounds the crew whips out the centreboard. Jump out and drag the boat up the beach.

Landing at a jetty (Fig. 12.5)

Sail towards the jetty slowly, controlling your speed with the sheets. Turn into the wind at the last moment.

If the 'ideal' position C is occupied, follow course D. As the boat turns into the wind, the crew goes forward and grabs the jetty. He can get onto it and tie up while the helmsman lowers the sails.

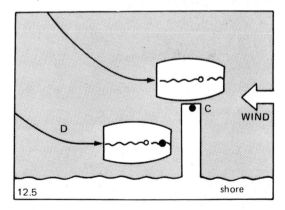

12.5   shore

45

13 Tuning

What is tuning?

Tuning is adjusting your boat to get the best combination of mast rake, sail shape and sail trim for the wind and sea conditions. The aim is to get maximum drive from the sails.

Remember that no two suits of sails are made exactly the same, so if you change a sail you will need to re-tune the rig.

The following points refer to the beat, which is where good tuning can help most.

TUNING ON LAND

Mast rake

Chock the boat level. Tie a weight (such as a large nut) to the aft end of the main halyard and let it swing level with the bottom of the mast. The distance between the weight and the bottom of the mast should be between 10 and 15 cm. If it isn't, adjust the shrouds and forestay until it is. Check that the mast does not lean to left or right.

Shrouds and forestay

For medium winds and flat water, tighten the rigging so that you can pull the middle of the fore-stay 15 cm to one side. For light winds and flat water, slacken the rigging so this distance becomes 20 cm. In strong winds and a chop the rigging should be bar tight—even then it will tend to slacken as the boat slams against the waves.

Jib

The jib is far more important than its size might indicate, as it does two jobs. Firstly, it develops drive of its own. Secondly, it deflects the wind over the leeward side of the mainsail. The greater the difference in the wind speeds over the leeward and windward sides of the mainsail, the greater the drive and lift.

To set up the jib correctly I suggest that you temporarily stick five pairs of telltales (12 cm lengths of wool) to the jib with sticky tape in the following way. Position three pairs approximately 15 cm from the leading edge (luff) and one-quarter, half and three-quarters of the way up the luff. Fix the remaining two pairs about 10 cm from the trailing edge (leech), one-third and two-thirds of the way up the leech.

Fully rig the boat and align it at an angle of 45° to the wind. Have friends hold the boat firm with the mainsail adjusted properly and the main-sheet pulled in hard as if beating. Hold the jib-sheet, using forefinger and thumb as a moveable fairlead, and find a position on the gunwale or deck where all the telltales fly horizontally. The leech of the jib should be as close to the mainsail as possible without backwinding the mainsail. The jib leech must be flat, not hooked, so the wind leaves the jib leech fast.

The person checking the telltales should be standing far enough away on the leeward side to see all the telltales at once. When the ideal position for the jibsheet is found, mark the spot as this will be the bearing edge of the fairlead. (At the time of writing some countries do not allow fairleads on the deck, so if in doubt check with your national association.)

Now, note the height of the jib tack and the wind strength. With the same fairlead position the jib tack should be lower in stronger winds, higher in lighter winds.

Finally, turn the boat slowly into the wind. The jib luff should lift (start to flap) a fraction before the mainsail does.

All telltales can now be removed except the lowest pair along the luff.

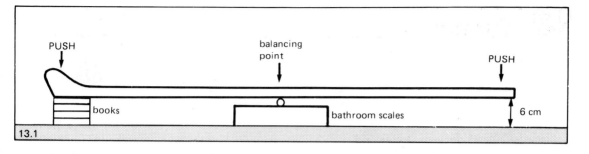

Weight	Suitable for
32 kg (70 lb)	heavy helmsman and crew, with flat luff in mainsail. Effective over a wide range of wind strength.
27 kg (60 lb)	less heavy helmsman and crew, with flat luff in mainsail. Effective over a wide range of wind strength.
23 kg (50 lb)	average helmsman and crew weight, with more luff round in mainsail. The gully behind the gaff will disappear when the wind fills the sail.
18 kg (40 lb)	lightweight helmsman and crew, but will limit sails to a small range of wind strengths to suit the luff round.
14 kg (30 lb)	Not suitable, as range of wind strengths very limited.

TUNING ON THE WATER

Mainsail

The amount of bend in the gaff and mast is important in relation to the shape of the mainsail and the total crew weight: the heavier the crew, the stiffer the gaff and mast must be. As most masts are metal there is less variation in bend than in the original wood masts, but the variation in the bend characteristics of the wooden gaffs is considerable. A simple method of measuring gaff bend is shown in Fig. 13.1.

With the gaff slot facing downwards, place the gaff on a set of bathroom scales so that the balancing point of the gaff rests on a small round spacer on the scales. Pack one end of the gaff so that the other end is 6 cm clear of the ground. Stand someone on each end of the gaff and read off the weight on the scales. The readings given in the table above provide a guide to the suitability of the gaff.

Higher pointing without loss of speed is possible if the luff of the mainsail is flat. (Wind must be coaxed round shallow bends—it objects, by stalling, to going round sharp bends.)

Balance

It is most important to find out if the boat is *balanced* (i.e. goes straight when sailed dead upright). To do so, sail the boat on a beat, making sure that it is level and that both sails are trimmed; the helmsman then puts his tiller hand over and around the tiller without touching it (but ready to correct immediately if need be). In medium winds the boat should go straight ahead without any tiller correction. If the boat turns into the wind, move the mast step forward, keeping the rake constant. If the mast step is already as far forward as the rules of measurement allow, reduce the aft rake of the mast. When beating upwind most helmsmen like to feel a 'pull' on the tiller ('weather helm')—remember that this is added drag, reducing upwind speed.

Halyards

Performance upwind is often lost by the main halyard stretching or slipping so that the gaff falls away from the mast. The tension on the mainsheet and kicking strap causes the gaff to bend, flattening the sail; creases appear by the gaff jaws and drive is lost. The gaff must be as tight as possible against the mast so that the gaff can just turn around the mast in the available wind strength.

The jib halyard must be tight enough so that there are no curves in the luff between hanks. The jib halyard is best set when on the run, when the mast is pushed forward. If a gully forms just behind the luff the halyard is too tight.

Sail controls

Adjustments to the kicking strap, downhaul and outhaul are discussed throughout this book. Some creases in your sails are inevitable, but many can be avoided by careful adjustments of these three controls and that all-important rope from the tack, around the mast and back.

In very light winds, when the downhaul should be slack, some small creases up the luff are permissible.

14 The spinnaker

The spinnaker is an extra sail used for reaching and running. You will be surprised at how much faster your boat will go when you are flying a spinnaker.

Spinnaker gear is discussed on pages 16-17. As I mentioned there, I use a net rather than a chute, so the following instructions refer to a net. If you use a chute, you should find the manoeuvres even easier, but your spinnaker will become distorted in the centre.

RAISING THE SPINNAKER

1 The crew puts the spinnaker pole in a handy position and unclips the spinnaker halyard from the gunwale (Fig. 14.1).

2 The helmsman starts to pull the spinnaker up.

The crew makes sure the sail comes out from under the net. If the spinnaker is launched on the windward side, the crew makes sure it goes forward of the forestay (this is vital). The crew clips the pole onto the tack of the spinnaker (*not* onto the guy)—Fig. 14.2.

3 The crew pushes the pole forwards (Fig. 14.3).

4 The crew clips the aft end of the pole onto the bracket on the mast (Fig. 14.4).

5 The crew hooks the support rod onto the eye on the foredeck, while the helmsman trims the spinnaker sheet and guy (Fig. 14.5).

6 The crew takes over the sheet and guy from the helmsman (Fig. 14.6). Both use their weight to balance the boat.

14.1

14.2

14.3

14.4

14.5

14.6

If it's blowing very hard, you may find it easier to turn onto a broad reach while pulling up the spinnaker. Get back on course as soon as you're under control.

REACHING WITH THE SPINNAKER

Trimming on a reach

The endless guy and sheet system makes trimming the spinnaker simple. As you pull the guy the sheet goes out and vice versa. The tensioner controls the tension on the sheet, and so affects the curve in the spinnaker.

Pull the guy until the luff of the spinnaker is about to collapse. You now have the spinnaker at its most efficient angle. Keep 'playing' the guy constantly so the luff just trembles.

The spinnaker pole should be set pointing upwards some 30° to open the luff of the spinnaker. The further aft the wind blows, the less this angle should be (the support rod makes this adjustment automatically).

Tighten the tensioner only enough to keep the sail full. Keeping the tensioner as slack as possible allows the spinnaker clew to come forward, bringing the drive of the sail forwards rather than sideways. The nearer your course is to the wind, the tighter the tensioner will need to be.

If you alter course towards the wind, you will eventually reach the point where the spinnaker will slow the boat down. It can still serve a useful purpose, however, if those around you are less experienced than you or have a fuller spinnaker. In trying to use their spinnakers the confusion may well slow them down more than you!

It is on a reach that a properly trimmed spinnaker pays the greatest dividend. For this reason a full-cut spinnaker is less effective than a flat one.

If a gust hits you, alter course away from the wind, easing both main and spinnaker sheets slightly. In this way you stay with the stronger wind a little longer. Get back on course when the gust has passed.

Reaching in light winds

To reduce the wetted area of the hull, heel the boat to leeward. This will also compensate for rudder drag, as a spinnaker tends to turn the boat to leeward and heeling to leeward corrects this tendency. If the water is flat, move your weight forward a little.

Reaching in medium winds

Be prepared to hike out when a stronger gust comes, but as long as you can cope with the increased strength of wind keep a straight course for the next buoy.

Reaching in strong winds

Both helmsman and crew should hike out, moving their weight aft. The spinnaker guy passes over the crew's body as he hikes so does not interfere with his movements.

When gusts come, bear off a little—you will plane fast and find the boat easier to control. Beware of boats to leeward of you because if you have no room to bear away a stronger gust may capsize you. If you have to bear away too often you may end up too low to make the next buoy while flying the spinnaker. In this case, take the spinnaker down in good time to fetch up to the buoy. This may well be faster than struggling to keep the boat upright and not planing.

RUNNING WITH THE SPINNAKER

Trimming on a run

Trim the guy in the same way as you do on a reach—so that the luff of the spinnaker is almost collapsing. The spinnaker boom will be nearly at right angles to the boat and horizontal. The tensioner should be slack.

You may be tempted to run by the lee (page 34) with the spinnaker up. Don't! The mainsail is larger than the spinnaker and its effect is more important. Running by the lee reduces the area of mainsail presented to the wind and thus reduces its efficiency. If you find you're running by the lee, either turn into the wind or gybe.

Running in light winds

If the wind is so light that the sails aren't filling, heel the boat to leeward. The crew should gently pull the spinnaker boom back in the hope of filling the sail. If the spinnaker collapses, push the boom forward and try again. The helmsman meanwhile should be forward, holding the main boom out. The helmsman and crew may exchange these jobs. The centreboard should only be 5 or 6 cm into the water.

Running in medium winds

Both helmsman and crew should be forward to reduce the wetted area of the hull, even to the extent of burying the bow 6 or 7 cm. The crew constantly trims the sail so that the luff is almost lifting. It's best for the crew to sit to leeward where he can give a sharp pull back on the sheet to fill the spinnaker if it collapses.

The helmsman meanwhile watches the burgee; if the wind shifts to leeward he can either turn into the wind or gybe, depending on where the next buoy is. He also steers to keep out of the windshadow of the boats behind.

The centreboard should be about 20 cm into the water. The spinnaker halyard can be released 10 to 15 cm. The spinnaker boom should be horizontal (if you can adjust it) to help pull the spinnaker out from the lee of the mainsail.

Running in strong winds

Helmsman and crew should sit on opposite gunwales to counteract rolling. If this doesn't kill the rolling, the centreboard should be lowered halfway down or even more. The boat will plane more easily if helmsman and crew are well back.

As a wave overtakes, move your weight forward in order to surf on the face of the wave. If you overtake a wave you will bury the bow in the next wave and stop, so be prepared to move your weight back quickly before this happens.

As lift occurs at right angles to the spinnaker on the run, the spinnaker halyard needs to be tight and the guy and sheet tensioner loose: the boat will then plane a little earlier, as the spinnaker helps to lift the bow out of the water.

GYBING THE SPINNAKER

Gybing the spinnaker is made easier by the endless sheet and guy system, which keeps the spinnaker in place when the crew's hands are busy. The support rod is also a help when gybing as it needs no attention.

Push the centreboard down before you start your gybe—this is essential.

The helmsman's job

Use your weight to balance the crew, who has to do most of the work during the gybe. In the photographs opposite, the wind is light so the helmsman is sitting to leeward.

Follow the instructions for gybing on page 38, but this time *you* should uncleat the jibsheet and set it on the new side. You can also trim the spinnaker after the gybe until the crew is ready to take over.

The crew's job

1 Trim the spinnaker as the boat turns onto a run (Fig. 14.7).

2 Let go of the sheet and guy and pull the mainsail over (Fig. 14.8). Duck under the boom and cross the boat.

3 The spinnaker is now behind the mainsail which takes the wind out of it. Unclip the spinnaker boom from the bracket on the mast (Fig. 14.9).

4 Clip this same end into the new tack of the spinnaker (Fig. 14.10).

5 Unclip the other end of the spinnaker boom from the old tack and clip it to the bracket on the mast (Fig. 14.11).

6 Trim the spinnaker (Fig. 14.12).

14.7

14.8

14.9

14.10

14.11

14.12

LOWERING THE SPINNAKER

Lowering on a reach

1 The helmsman balances the boat as the crew comes inboard. In strong winds you may have to bear away to balance the boat more easily (Fig. 14.13).

2 The crew unhooks the boom support from the foredeck (Fig. 14.14).

3 The crew unclips the spinnaker boom from the mast and the tack of the spinnaker. He grabs the support rod and spinnaker boom in his outside hand and drops both on the sidetank inside the shroud (Fig. 14.15).

4 The helmsman dodges the aft end of the spinnaker boom and support rod (sometimes!) and releases the spinnaker halyard. The crew gathers the foot of the spinnaker, pulling it either to windward of the forestay (as in Fig. 14.16) or under the jib (he chooses the method that will give a leeward hoist on the next spinnaker leg).

5 The crew tucks the spinnaker under the net (Fig. 14.17). In strong winds the crew does not go forward so soon but pulls the guy so that the spinnaker comes into his hands and then quickly leans forward to push the gathered spinnaker under the forward edge of the net.

6 The crew clips the spinnaker halyard to the gunwale (Fig. 14.18), then returns to his normal position and takes the jibsheet.

Lowering on a run

This is essentially the same as lowering on a reach except that the helmsman will be on the leeward side of the boat as the manoeuvre begins. Two further points:

● Make sure the centreboard is right down. This gives the crew a chance to get across the boat to counteract rolling.

● Heel the boat to windward. This stops the boat broaching (turning violently into the wind) as the spinnaker is lowered.

14.13

14.16

14.14

14.15

14.17

14.18

15 Racing

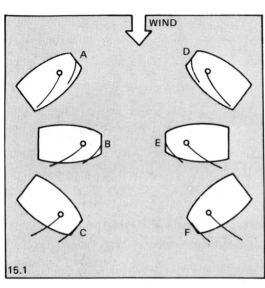

WIND

15.1

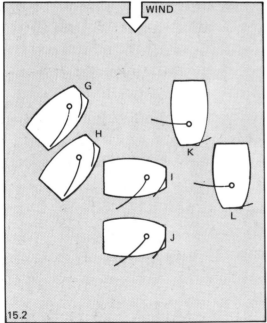

WIND

15.2

THE RULES

A full discussion of the rules is outside the scope of this book. For the cautious beginner, a few key rules will keep him out of trouble in most cases.

Boats meeting on opposite tacks

A boat is either on a port tack or a starboard tack. It is on a port tack if the wind is blowing over its port side. In Fig. 15.1, boats A, B and C are on port tack; boats D, E and F are on starboard tack.

A port tack boat must keep clear of a starboard tack boat.

D, E and F have right of way over A, B and C, who must keep clear.

Boats meeting on the same tack

If the boats are overlapped (i.e. if the bow of the following boat is ahead of a line at right angles to the stern of the leading boat) the following rule applies:

A windward boat shall keep clear of a leeward boat.

In Fig. 15.2, G must keep clear of H, I must keep clear of J and K must keep clear of L.

If the boats are *not* overlapped (Fig. 15.3):

A boat clear astern shall keep clear of a boat clear ahead.

M is overtaking and is not allowed to sail into the back of N.

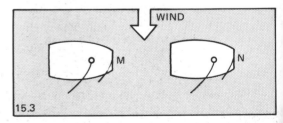

WIND

15.3

56

Boats meeting at marks

An outside boat shall give each boat overlapping it on the inside room to round or pass the mark.

O must give P room to go round the mark on the inside. P must get his overlap on O before O's bow reaches an imaginary circle of radius two boat's lengths from the mark (Fig. 15.4). In Fig.

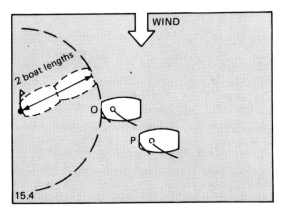

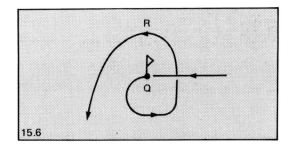

(from point Q to point R) (Fig. 15.6).

If you hit another boat and reckon you're in the right, protest by flying a red flag (a small piece of cloth clothespegged to your shroud is the simplest method). Argue your case in the protest room afterwards.

If you hit another boat and are in the wrong, you must either retire or, if the rules allow (they usually do), make a 720° turn. In effect, you have to tack, gybe, tack again and gybe again—then sail on (Fig. 15.7).

15.5, the boats are rounding the buoy to starboard (clockwise). The boat nearest the camera has the right to turn inside the other boat.

Note that this rule does not apply at starts (see next page).

Penalties

If you hit a mark, you must go round it again. You have no rights while you are re-rounding

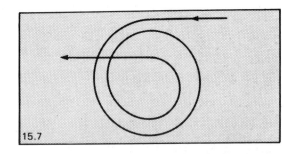

THE LINE START

The start is the most important part of the race. If you get a bad start, you have to overtake everyone to win—while you're battling past the opposition, the leaders are sailing further ahead. If you get a good start, you're sailing in clear air.

How is a race started?

Most races are started on a beat. The race committee sets an (imaginary) start line, usually between the mast of the committee boat (A) and a buoy (B) (Fig. 15.8). They often lay another buoy (C), which does not have to be on the line. Boats are not allowed to sail between C and A.

Ten minutes before the start the class flag (or a white shape) is raised on the committee boat and a gun is fired.

Five minutes before the start the blue peter (or a blue shape) is raised and a gun is fired.

At the start, both flags are lowered (or a red shape is raised) and a gun is fired.

Boats must be behind the start line when the starting gun is fired. Your aim is to be just behind the line, sailing at full speed, when the gun fires.

How can I get a good start?

Set your watch at the ten-minute gun, and check it at the five-minute gun.

During the last few minutes, avoid the 'danger' areas X and Y. From X you cannot get on to the start line because the boats to leeward have right of way. Boat D, for example, will be forced the wrong side of buoy C. In Y you are bound to pass the wrong side of buoy B. Boat F has this problem.

Don't go too far from the line—30 metres is plenty. A wall of boats builds up on the line in the last two minutes, and you must be in that wall. If you're behind it, not only can you not get in, but your wind is cut off by the wall.

Aim to be two boat lengths behind the line with 20 seconds to go. Control your speed by backing the jib. Keep the boat creeping forward

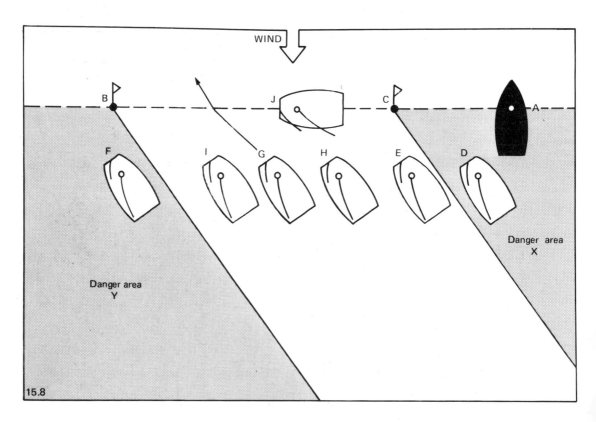

15.8

as slowly as you can—most of the sails will be flapping. With five seconds to go, you should be one length behind the line. Free the jib, pull in the jib and mainsheets, hike out and start beating. You should cross the line just after the gun with full speed. Boat G has followed this advice.

What about the other boats?

It's important to watch out for other boats as you line up to start. G has right of way over H, but must keep clear of I. As you line up, keep turning into the wind a little. This keeps you away from the boat to leeward—it also opens up a nice 'hole' to leeward that you can sail down into at the start (for extra speed).

Don't reach down the line with 15 seconds to go like boat J. You will have no rights over G, H and I who will sail into you. If you're too early, let the sails out in good time and slow down.

Which end of the line should I start?

In the diagram opposite the wind is at right angles to the start line. In this case it doesn't matter where you start—the middle is as good as anywhere.

Usually, however, the wind is not at right angles to the line. You can find out what it's doing by sailing down the line on a reach with the jib flapping. Adjust the mainsail so the front just flaps (Fig. 15.9).

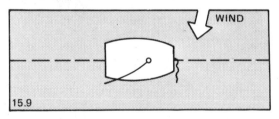

15.9

Keeping the mainsheet in the same position, tack and reach back down the line. In Fig. 15.10,

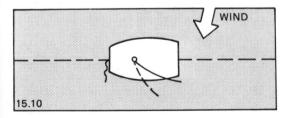

15.10

the mainsail will now be too far in—you will have to let the mainsheet out to make it flap. This indicates the wind is blowing from the starboard end of the line—and you should start at this end.

How do I make a starboard end start?

Sail slowly, and as close to the wind as possible, so you will reach the windward end of the line with the gun (Fig. 15.11). Boats to windward

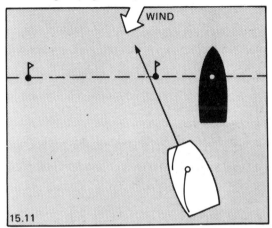

15.11

have no rights and are forced out. Boats to leeward can't touch you—you are already sailing as close to the wind as possible.

How do I make a port end start?

Keep near the port end of the line (Fig. 15.12).

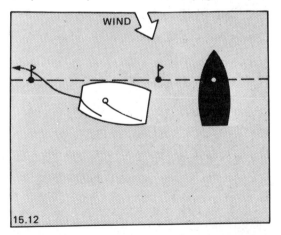

15.12

Aim to cross as near the buoy as possible. Tack on to port tack as soon as you can clear the fleet.

THE GATE START

A gate start is made by crossing the wake of a boat called the pathfinder which is beating on port tack in front of the fleet. In theory everyone has an equally good start, because the earlier you start the further you have to sail.

The pathfinder, who is selected by the race committee from among the competitors, waits near the committee boat while the usual sound and flag signals are made. About one minute before the start the pathfinder sets off on port tack, accompanied by two motor boats, the gate boat and guard boat, to protect it from overenthusiastic competitors. (See Fig. 15.13.) A few seconds before the start a free-floating buoy is dropped over the back of the gate boat to mark the left-hand end of the line. After the start competitors (on starboard tack) pass closely behind the gate boat (Fig. 15.14). The line gradually lengthens, and the boats start one at a time. A late start is no disadvantage, since the pathfinder is sailing up the beat for you while you're waiting.

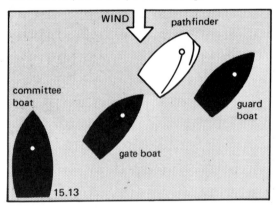

15.13

How can I get a good start?

You need to know the course the pathfinder will take. So, with about four minutes to go, begin beating on port tack from the committee boat. After two or three minutes bear away onto a reach, then tack and wait with your sails flapping (like boat G in Fig. 15.14). Watch for the pathfinder, and control your speed so that you beat slowly up to the stern of the guard boat. As you go behind it, pick up speed by bearing away slightly and hiking. Then beat, flat out, to pass just behind the stern of the gate boat.

NEVER reach towards the guard boat like boat F. You have no rights over boats D and E who will push you into the guard boat or gate boat. If you hit either, you will be disqualified. If you find yourself in boat F's position, try to tack onto port and bear away. When you're ready, tack back onto starboard and try again. If all else fails, point into the wind and stop!

How can I recover from a bad start?

If you start too far from the gate boat, your only option is to sail through the gate, then tack onto port and sail behind the whole fleet to the right-hand side of the course. If that turns out to be the best side, you could find yourself ahead at the windward mark!

Where should I start?

Start late if you're slower than the pathfinder, if you think the pathfinder will hit a permanent header (see page 62) or if the tide is more favourable to the right of the course.

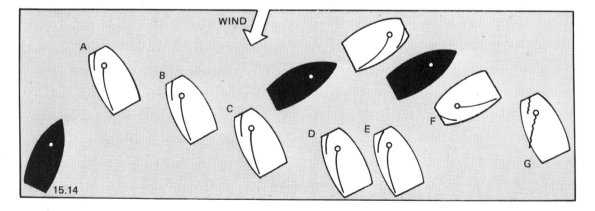

15.14

THE BEAT

After the tension of the start, it's important to settle down and concentrate on sailing hard.

What about other boats?

A boat when beating casts a 'wind shadow'—shown in Fig. 15.15. It also creates an area of disturbed air to windward due to the wind being deflected by the sails; the air behind the boat is also disturbed.

You should therefore avoid sailing just to windward of another boat, behind it or in its wind shadow. In the diagram, boat B should either tack or bear away to clear its wind. Boats D and F should both tack.

Which way should I go?

You may have to modify your course to take account of tides and windshifts, but your first aim should be to make reasonably long tacks to start with, shortening them as you approach the windward mark.

Don't sail into the area indicated by the shaded part of Fig.15.16—if you do, you will have to reach in to the buoy and will lose valuable time and distance. Stay inside the lay lines—these are the paths you would sail when beating to hit the windward mark.

For safety's sake, arrange your tacks so that you come in to the mark on starboard tack. This gives you right of way over those approaching on port tack.

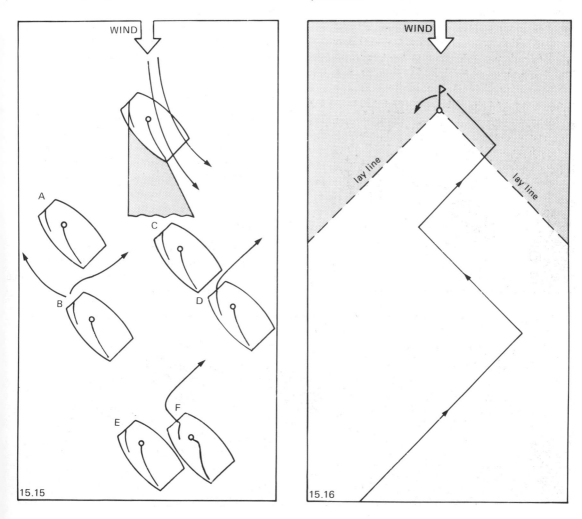

15.15

15.16

Windshifts

Once you are confident at beating and can tack efficiently, you are ready to start using windshifts.

The wind constantly alters in direction about its mean. Some of the shifts are more pronounced and last longer than others—it is these that you have to spot and use.

In shifty winds, stay close to the middle of the beat. Tack each time the wind heads you (forces you to alter course *away* from the mark). In Fig. 15.17, the boat takes no account of windshifts. Note how little progress it makes compared with the boat in Fig. 15.18, which tacks each time the wind heads it.

The main problem is to differentiate between a real shift and a short-lived change in the wind. For that reason, sail on into each shift for five or ten seconds to make sure it's going to last.

If a header lasts that long, tack.

If you find yourself tacking too often, or are confused, sail on one tack for a while until you're sure what the wind is doing. Remember that you lose at least a boat's length each time you tack, so there has to be a good reason to do so.

How can I get up the beat faster?

● Follow the tips for fast beating on page 27, 'Going faster'.

● Keep your wind clear.

● Watch for windshifts.

● Keep near the middle of the course.

● Practise tacking.

● Get fit—you can then hike harder.

15.17

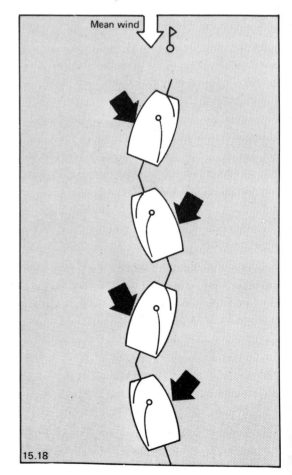

15.18

THE REACH

As you bear away round the windward mark, turn slowly, moving your weight back and letting out the sheets. Pull the centreboard half up as you turn.

What course should I steer?

The quickest way down the reach is a straight line from one mark to the next. However, if your rivals let you sail this course, you're lucky! The problem is that overtaking boats (e.g. A in Fig. 15.19) push up to windward. The boats to leeward (e.g. B) get nervous about their wind being stolen and steer high also. The result is that everyone sails an enormous arc (X), losing ground on the leaders.

You have to decide whether or not to go on the 'great circle'; the alternative is to sail a leeward path (Y). You have to go down far enough to avoid the blanketing effect of the boats to windward—but usually you will sail a shorter distance than they do. You will also get the inside turn at the gybe mark. You can go for the leeward route on the second reach too, but this time you will be on the outside at the turn.

How can I get down the reach faster?

- Follow the tips for fast reaching on page 22, 'Going faster'.

- Keep your wind clear.

- Sail the shortest route.

- Go for the inside turn at marks.

- Use the spinnaker if the wind is on the beam or further aft. *Don't* use the spinnaker on a reach if you're likely to capsize!

Starting the next beat

As you approach the leeward mark, tighten the downhaul and outhaul and push down the centreboard. Steer round the mark so that you leave it very close (like boat C). Don't come in to the mark close (like boat D) or you'll start the beat well to leeward of your rivals.

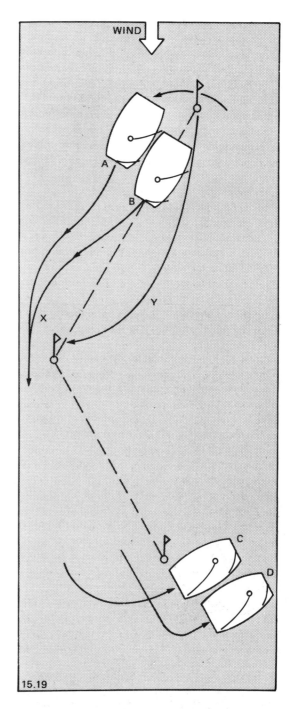

15.19

THE RUN

In strong winds, take your time as you bear away on to a run. Pull the centreboard half up, sit back and adjust the sheets as you turn. If the boat starts to roll, steer a straight course and pull in the mainsheet a little. Continue to bear away when the boat is under control.

What course should I steer?

The quickest route is a straight line to the leeward mark (Fig. 15.20).

In very strong winds, you may not be able to control the boat on a straight downwind run. An alternative is to follow course Z, wearing round (see page 38) rather than gybing at the midpoint.

The presence of other boats may also prevent your steering a straight course. Boat F is blanketed by boat E—it can escape by steering to one side (course M or N). Other things being equal, N would be better since it gives the inside turn at the next mark.

Boat E is correct to blanket F in this way. E can attack from a range of up to four boat's lengths; it can sail right up behind F, turning to one side at the last moment to overtake. E must, of course, keep clear of F during this manoeuvre.

Watch out for boats still beating, especially when running on port tack. Alter course in good time to avoid them—a last-minute turn could capsize you.

What about crowding at the leeward mark?

It often happens that several boats arrive at the leeward mark together. The inside berth is the place to aim for—H, I and J have to give G room to turn inside them. If you're in J's position, it's better to slow down and wait to turn close to the buoy rather than sail round the outside of the pack. Try to anticipate this situation, and slow down and move across to the inside in good time. Try to get G's position.

As you get near the leeward mark, tighten the downhaul and push the centreboard down. Turn slowly and aim to leave the mark close (course O). You will need to pull in a good length of mainsheet as you round this mark—pull it in with your front hand, then clamp it under the thumb

of your tiller hand while you grab the mainsheet to pull in the next length.

How do I get down the run faster?

- Follow the 'Going faster' tips on p. 36.
- Keep your wind clear.
- Go for the inside turn at the leeward mark.
- Use the spinnaker.

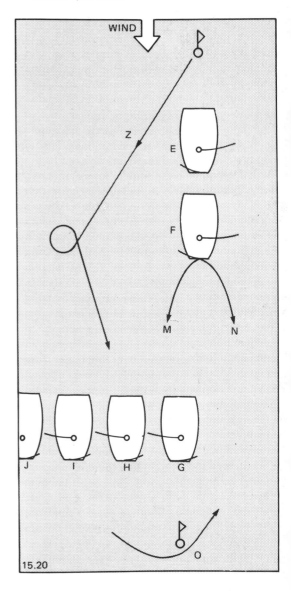

15.20